The **Lazy**

Refuge

Finding a Purpose
and a Path

Ringu Tulku

Number 3 in the Lazy Lama series

Published in 2000

Bodhicharya Publications
28 Carrick Drive
Coatbridge
Lanarkshire
Scotland ML5 1JZ
e-mail: margaret@bodhicharya.org

ISBN 0 9534489 2 4

Edited by Cait Collins
Design by Jude Tarrant
Line drawings by Robin Bath
Front cover photo by Robin Bath
Back cover photo by Johanna Lamby

Printed in England by Print Plus, Hereford.

Editor's Note

This is the third of the **Lazy Lama's** uniquely relaxed looks at Buddhist practice. It is based on a talk given by Ringu Tulku Rinpoche in Chichester, England in the summer of 2000.

There are many books about Buddhism available in English nowadays and words from Asian languages such as Sanskrit and Tibetan are gradually being adopted into the language: 'buddha' and 'lama' can be found now in almost any dictionary. Certain conventions are emerging as teachers and translators take on the challenge of communicating concepts in another language. One such convention is the distinction between 'the Buddha' with a capital B, usually meaning the historical Buddha Shakyamuni, and 'a buddha' with a small b, usually meaning any fully enlightened being. I have followed that convention here. I have also used the initial capital for Buddha and for Lama when referring to either specifically as an object of refuge. I have chosen to spell Sanskrit words phonetically rather than using diacritical marks.

I would like to thank Ringu Tulku Rinpoche for his boundless kindness and unfailing patience, and for communicating the Dharma with a warmth and spontaneity that brings the teachings to life and imparts to us a glimpse of how it is, and how it would be, if only we'd let it. I'd also like to thank the students of Bodhicharya Buddhist Group for requesting and arranging the talk in Chichester; Jude Tarrant for design and technological expertise; Robin Bath for the drawings and the front cover photo; and Norma Levine for help with editing and for making irreverent jokes.

Cait Collins
Sussex, September 2000

Refuge

The concept of 'refuge' is fundamental in Buddhism. It's connected with something that I think also applies in a way within every spiritual tradition, and even to every individual person: our need to find a purpose in our lives.

What is it that I really want? What is the highest goal that I want to realise? What is my ultimate dream? Asking myself these kind of questions can enable me to identify my purpose, whatever it is that I want most to achieve, that would benefit myself and others.

Of course we could probably all agree on a basic wish: I don't want anything negative to happen to me and I don't want any sufferings or problems or pain; and I would like to find peace and joy and enjoy only good experiences. If only there could be no suffering, no problems, no pain, and only lasting happiness, peace, and joy – that's the basic wish we all share, isn't it?

Now the question comes up as to whether that's really possible. Could there be any possibility of our actually having that kind of a state of mind, or experience?

1

Could the sufferings that we encounter in our lives be eradicated; could the problems be solved?

Here I think we can find something encouraging to consider: according to the Buddhist teachings, based on the experience of the Buddha – and maybe also in accordance with the experience of all the great spiritual masters of the great spiritual traditions in the world – there is a possibility of finding a way to free ourselves from the miseries we experience.

The Buddha talked about this in terms of the Four Noble Truths: he observed that we experience problems and sufferings, and that these sufferings have a cause or causes; and that the causes can be rectified, and therefore the problems can cease. So we can see in this way that there is a possibility of an experience, or a realisation, that is available to anybody. In Buddhism this realisation is termed 'enlightenment', or 'bodhi'. Bodhi is a Sanskrit word based on the verb root bodh, which means to know, understand, see clearly, or awaken; the root bodh then goes to the noun bodhi, meaning knowledge, understanding, wisdom, or awakening.

This understanding or awakening is not something that can be achieved by only one person, like the historical Buddha, the Buddha Shakyamuni. In Buddhism we sometimes refer to the Buddha Shakyamuni as the tathagata; in fact the Buddha used to call himself the tathagata. Tatha means 'like them', while gata means 'gone'; so tathagata means 'one who has walked the same way that others have passed'. This means that he isn't the first buddha, but that he has experienced and understood in the same way as other great enlightened beings of the past have done. Therefore becoming a buddha is not an achievement that is totally new or unique to one person, but is possible for every being who understands clearly and sees or experiences directly the way things are; and everyone has the potential to do that.

So this is the main understanding from the Buddhist perspective: there is a possibility to free ourselves and become enlightened. It isn't easy for us to understand this. How strongly we can understand it and have confidence in it depends on many factors, but I think we can begin to develop some confidence based on a little bit of an understanding or feeling that things can change, and that something can be transformed within us. In a way, there must be some basic confidence or feeling in us that some kind of transformation is possible in order for us to do anything at all, otherwise why would we do anything? And anybody who tries to work on a spiritual path or attempts any kind of self-improvement must have a certain feeling that transformation is possible. If we didn't think there was any possibility of bringing about change then there would be no sense in our doing anything.

From a Buddhist point of view, we can describe what it means to be a buddha very simply: we can say that a buddha is somebody who has increased or developed his or her wisdom and compassion fully, to the utmost. We can describe it in a more complicated way if we like – we can expand the description to fill many books! – but we can also describe it as simply as this: whoever has fully developed their compassion and wisdom can be called a buddha.

How can we know that it's possible for each one of us to develop our compassion and wisdom? The traditional answer is that all beings have within them the seedling of compassion and wisdom. Even the most cruel, unkind person, however evil he or she might appear to be, has a certain soft corner for somebody at some time, and where there is a little bit of compassion, a little bit of love, there is no reason why that can't be developed and matured. In the same way, every being – especially every human being – however dull or confused he or she might be, has some sense of right and wrong, and that is the basis of wisdom. So where there is a little bit of a certain quality present, we can cultivate it and increase it; and where there is the basis or the seedling of compassion and wisdom in us we can develop that. In that way transformation is possible for all beings.

Now we can begin to think about this in terms of the Buddhist idea of refuge. In Buddhism we talk about refuge with regard to the Buddha, the Dharma, and the Sangha, and the definition of a Buddhist is a person who takes refuge in these Three Jewels, as they're called. We say that a person becomes a Buddhist by taking refuge, but it would be a mistake to think that taking refuge is only for beginners. It's actually the whole practice of Buddhism.

The term 'going for refuge' can sound odd to those who aren't familiar with it. For example, it can have the connotation of seeking a place of refuge, like a refugee seeking a safe place; or when we say, 'I take refuge in the Buddha', it can sound as if we're saying, 'O Buddha, please save me', as though we were pleading or praying. But in fact going for refuge isn't like either of those things. Rather it's more like making a decision, based on the conviction that there is a potential for buddhahood or enlightenment within me and that it's possible for me to realise or awaken to this potential: I decide that I want to do that and I make a commitment to take that as my goal.

The Buddha refuge

It's said that if you go for refuge to the Buddha, Dharma, and Sangha, then you are a Buddhist, and as long as you are doing that then you are practising Buddhism. But what does it mean, to go for refuge to the Buddha? It's not a matter of praying, 'O Buddha, please have mercy on me, please save me,' and then thinking, 'OK, that's finished; now I'm OK. I've said my prayers, so now I can do whatever I like.' That's not the idea! That may be praying to the Buddha but it's not going for refuge to the Buddha. Going for refuge to the Buddha is something else: it's finding a direction, finding a purpose. It's saying: 'I want to become free of all my sufferings and find lasting happiness and joy, and I want to achieve this for the benefit of all sentient beings, so that I will be in a position to help others do the same. It's possible for me to do that, and therefore I will do it; and that is my real, ultimate goal.' Going for refuge to the Buddha means that we have that sense of direction very clearly, and we maintain that direction however quickly or slowly we may travel along the path.

In saying that we want to be free of all our sufferings and find lasting peace and happiness, we are acknowledging the possibility of being able to achieve this goal. That's why we need to have some understanding of the Four Noble Truths as the basis for our taking refuge. There is suffering, and there are the causes of suffering; and if I can understand that these causes are changeable, or can be removed, then I can know that there is a possibility of changing my experience. If I understand that, then I can have confidence in the possibility of being able to achieve my goal. Even if I don't yet have the total experience, from my present understanding and whatever little experience I already have, I can see the possibility of freeing myself.

Now in order to discuss this properly we'll have to go a little into some of the basic Buddhist understanding and philosophy.

We all want happiness, but too much wanting is itself a problem, isn't it? I want to be happy, successful, healthy, and popular, but because I want these things so much, then even if I achieve them I find I still have a problem. Due to my wanting them so much, I have a fear or dread of losing them, and because of this fear I'm not completely happy; therefore I'm still suffering. That fear is itself a kind of suffering. And then of course, when something actually happens that I don't like, I will fear and dislike what's happening, and the more I fear it and dislike it, the more I will suffer.

According to the Buddhist understanding, the basis of the problem lies in our present way of experiencing our existence. I experience my existence in terms of 'I', and then relate to everything else as 'other'. Because of that view, I have to judge everything I encounter according to how it relates to me: either it's good for me or not good for me, friendly or not friendly. And because I see everything as either good or not good, I react to it with either attachment or aversion. If it's nice, I want it and I must run after it; or, if it's not so nice, I don't want it and must get rid of it or run away from it. In the process of reacting in this way we're always in some kind of conflict, always struggling, as we're continuously either running after or away from something. We're always agitated. How can we ever find peace, if everything we encounter is seen as either something to obtain or something to get rid of? We can never rest, because it's like that with everything we meet.

We can see in this way that the source of the

problem can be identified as aversion-attachment, based on the way I view myself in relation to everything else. My sense of self and of the real-ness of things is very strong. But, if we look into it deeply, it's very difficult to pinpoint exactly where 'I' end and 'other' begins. For example, I can say, 'This is me' while pointing to my body: 'This body is me, and beyond that is other'; but, if I look more deeply at the body in terms of its parts, I can see that it's not so simple. For example, my hand is part of my body, and I can say, 'This is my hand'; but if I lose my hand, or if I imagine losing my hand, then somehow my hand is not me any more. And in a way it wasn't ever really me, because it was 'my hand', as though it belonged to me. And it's like that with all the components of the body, right down to smallest cells.

If we think of the body as just 'my body', then where is this 'me' that is the owner of the body? Just as this body is not one indivisible thing but is based on many parts, so this 'me' is not really one thing but is a concept based on many things.

What I call 'me' is my body and my mind: there's nothing else. Although my body seems to be a very solid unitary thing, in fact it's composed of many parts and elements and is changing all the time. What I call my mind is my awareness; it's that which knows 'this is me' and 'this is other'. But what is the nature of this awareness? If we go deeply into it we see that our awareness, or consciousness, can't be found. Some people say that consciousness is the brain, or a function of the brain, but the brain is local, limited in space and time, while the mind is not local, not limited. With the mind you can see everything; if your mind is very clear it can see through space and time. So, although it's functioning through the brain at the moment, the mind can't be limited to the brain. Consciousness is subtle, it isn't something you can find or grasp. And if there's nothing to find or hold onto, then there's nothing to be destroyed.

As we continue looking carefully, we find that at the end of what we call 'me', then starts what we call 'mine'; and these two are closely related. Sometimes 'mine' even hurts more than 'me'. For example, if I own something I value greatly, such as a watch which I like very much, and it breaks, I have a pain in my heart!

We can see in this way that, although we have a very strong habitual identification of ourselves and everything else, if we look at it more deeply or more philosophically it can't be as easily defined as we thought. Although it's difficult for us to see it at the moment, we can understand that our very strong sense of the clear-cut identity of 'me' is really no more than our own concept. It's not that we don't exist! Nor is it that there's some kind of undifferentiated oneness. We're not trying to deny that things exist, but rather to understand the *way* in which they exist – their nature, you can say. And when we really investigate carefully, we discover that there are no ultimately identifiable, completely independent, self-existent entities. Everything we experience, everything that appears, including our bodies and our minds, is of the nature of impermanence and interdependence. It's a bit like our experience in dreams: dream-objects can be seen and touched, even broken. They appear vividly and seem very real. But when we wake up we realise they weren't really there.

Now the point of going into all this is in order to understand that our habitual way of reacting with only aversion-attachment isn't inevitable. It's possible to stop this process of compulsively running after and running away from what we perceive as 'other' in relation to 'me'. All our fear and attachment are coming from the thought that 'I' can be harmed or destroyed, but, if we can gain an understanding of our true nature, we will see there is really nothing to be destroyed. Then the fear will dissolve, and with it the attachment and aversion, and then there will be no need to run away from or run after anything.

We need to understand here that attachment and love are not at all the same. Attachment is created by fear, while love is created without fear. When we are free of fear we are free to experience love and compassion. In fact we find that compassion always accompanies wisdom – wisdom in this context meaning understanding the way things really are. In Buddhism we always talk about wisdom and compassion together. When we see very deeply that our true nature is such that there's nothing to be destroyed and nothing to be grasped, then there's no need to be afraid, no need to keep struggling with everything around us. There's no need to be selfish or self-seeking or to fight to get things for ourselves, so we're free to work for the benefit of others. When we lose our fear, there is compassion. So wisdom and compassion are related, and true compassion comes only from wisdom.

Wisdom is an important word here. It can be difficult to imagine what it would be like to be free from aversion-attachment, and sometimes people think it must mean a state of equanimity or dullness. But according to the Buddha it's actually an experience of great clarity and vibrancy, which is why terms like wisdom, clear light, and luminosity are used to describe it.

When we have done away with our basic underlying fear, that's freedom, liberation. And when wisdom and compassion are fully realised, that's enlightenment, right there. Buddhahood isn't something to be achieved or gained from outside. That's why it's called enlightenment, or realisation, which means seeing something that was always there but had been overlooked. We didn't realise it was so, but now we see the truth, the way it is; that's a realisation.

We can see therefore that it's not impossible to become free of our suffering, because the solution is an inner solution. We're not talking about trying to change the world and eliminate whatever we don't like, but about changing our own way of perceiving and our own way of reacting.

So now to explore the possibility of working towards this realisation becomes very important, because that's where the possibility of finding lasting peace and happiness lies. It's what I want for myself and for others, and it's what I want to aim for. It's something I must actually experience, not just intellectually think about. It's not an easy task, because my way of seeing and reacting has become so ingrained that it's become habitual, almost second nature, and it won't just disappear in a moment, but to work towards this realisation can become my long-term goal.

That's what is meant by going for refuge to the Buddha: understanding the possibility of finding freedom within myself, and therefore wanting it for myself and for others, and taking that as my purpose. Discovering a purpose is maybe the most important thing we can do. Whatever we're doing, if we have a purpose, if we have a dream, then we can find a way. But if we have no purpose we don't know where we are or where we're going; we're lost. That's why, from the Buddhist point of view, this is the first and most important step.

This understanding which enables us to find our direction is also based on the experience of the Buddha himself. The fact that Buddha Shakyamuni and other great beings have achieved this goal provides us with an historical precedent or example. We can take the buddhas as our teachers. The real going for refuge to the Buddha includes both our own inner conviction in the possibility of enlightenment and our wanting to realise this, and our acceptance of the buddhas of the past, like Buddha Shakyamuni and other enlightened beings, as our examples and guides on an outer level.

The Dharma Refuge

Now when we take refuge in the Buddha, then we naturally have to take refuge in the Dharma, because the Dharma is the way or the path shown by the Buddha. We can say that if the Buddha is the teacher, then the Dharma is his teaching; or, if the Buddha is the person who has travelled along the path, then the Dharma is the road map he has drawn for us to follow.

There's a traditional story I like to tell which I think illustrates this point well.

There was a man who frequently attended the Buddha's teachings in Banaras, over a period of many years.

One day he came to the Buddha and said: 'I have a question for you.'

'OK,' said the Buddha, 'What is your question?'

'Well, I've been coming to your teachings for a long time, and I like what you say very much. But I see that although many people come to your teachings, and one or two really seem to change and attain some tremendous realisation, still it seems to me that many people remain unchanged. Why is that?'

'Where do you come from?' asked the Buddha. 'You don't sound as though you're from Banaras; your dialect is different.'

'I'm from Gaya,' the man replied.

'Well,' said the Buddha, 'in that case you must go to Gaya very often.'

'Yes, my family is there; I go back quite often.'

'So you must know the way to Gaya from Banaras very well.'

'Of course. I know the way to Gaya as though it were written on my palm.'

'In that case there must be many people who know that you know the way to Gaya.'

'Oh yes; all my friends know that I know the way

to Gaya.'

'So do people come to you to ask for directions to Gaya?'

'Yes; many people come and ask me to tell them how to get to Gaya.'

'Do you tell them?'

'Why not? I tell them every detail. There's no secret about it.'

'And everybody who asks you for the way to Gaya – do they all reach Gaya?'

'No; only those who actually complete the journey arrive there. The rest of them don't.'

'It's the same with me,' said the Buddha. 'I've been to enlightenment, and I know the way. People know I've been there, and they know I know the way, so they ask me how to get there. I tell them all I know; why not? There's no secret; I tell them everything. But only those who actually make the journey arrive there; otherwise they don't.'

It's like that: the Dharma is the way. It's the experience of the Buddha, or of anybody who has explored their way to enlightenment. There's not just one way; there are many ways. Anything that helps us to work on our understanding and our finding our true nature is the way. Dharma practice includes any method that helps us work towards this awakening. The practice is the Dharma. When we go for refuge to the Dharma, we're making a decision to try to understand and learn the methods by which we can become enlightened, and to try to practise in order to bring them into our experience. That's going for refuge to the Dharma: resolving to study the way, and to practise it.

The Dharma can be described in terms of two aspects: the teaching or scriptural Dharma and the Dharma of experience or realisation. The teaching Dharma consists of the teachings, in the sutras and tantras, of the Buddha and other great masters. The Buddha gave his followers guidance: 'If you do this, you will get this result,' and that's called the teaching Dharma, because it's a guide; it's the road map. But that's not the real Dharma; the real Dharma is the experience. There's a difference between talking about something and actually experiencing it. The Dharma of experience has to depend on the teaching Dharma, maybe, but the teaching Dharma is not the whole of the Dharma. If we listen to and understand the teaching Dharma and then put it into practice, we will experience it, and that's the real Dharma which will transform us. The teaching Dharma alone doesn't transform us, and unless we're transformed we're not really practising the Dharma.

The Sangha Refuge

Then, in order fully to go for refuge to the Dharma, we find that we need to go for refuge to the Sangha, because the real experience of the Dharma comes from the Sangha. The Sangha includes all the beings who actually have some experience of Dharma. It's very broad. The Buddha is also included in the Sangha, as someone who has realisation of the Dharma. We can receive the Dharma and gain understanding of the Dharma only from the

Sangha because the Dharma of experience can be found only in the beings who have some experience of it. We can read books, of course, but that isn't the same as an experience of Dharma; we need to receive this from experienced people. And the realisation is the important thing, because enlightenment is an experience, not just a theory or concept or intellectual idea.

If we understand that we go for refuge to the Sangha because we would like to understand and practise the Dharma, we can see that our taking refuge in the Sangha has two implications. Firstly, we want to associate with and learn from the beings who have some understanding or experience of the Dharma; and, secondly, on a more mundane level, we want to try to create an encouraging environment for ourselves and others. As human beings we are very changeable and can be easily influenced; we tend to be influenced by the people we associate with, for good or for ill. For example, if we stay with people who smoke we ourselves are more likely to smoke than if we spend time with non-smokers. So, in the beginning especially, it's not enough just to promise ourselves that we're going to practise the Dharma; we need actually to do something about creating the environment to support our resolve. If we are constantly in circumstances where the people around us are behaving in ways that are incompatible with our intention, we may find ourselves being influenced so that our resolve declines. We need consciously to put ourselves in a situation that encourages us in our Dharma-resolve, rather than allowing ourselves to be negatively influenced. It doesn't mean we have to avoid people who aren't Buddhists, or whose behaviour is not so positive, simply that we should take care to avoid being harmfully influenced. So going for refuge to the Sangha includes making an effort towards establishing a conducive environment for our Dharma practice.

So taking refuge means first identifying our purpose and then taking steps towards fulfilling that purpose. First we must understand the possibility of finding freedom, and identify that as a worthwhile and attainable aim, and affirm our intention to work towards attaining it. That's the refuge in the Buddha. Secondly, we decide we are going to learn and practise the methods which will transform us and bring us to that attainment; that's the Dharma refuge. And thirdly, we try to associate with the people who can help us to study and practise the Dharma, and we try to create a positive environment and conducive circumstances to encourage us in a positive way. That's the Sangha refuge.

We can see how taking refuge in the Three Jewels encompasses the entire path; all Buddhist practice is included in refuge. Therefore it's said that taking refuge is the definitive act of a Buddhist, meaning that it's the basis of Buddhist practice – not so much in the sense of Buddhist practice as a religion, but more as an inner journey, a spiritual journey. When we say 'Buddha' we're not just referring to the historical Buddha or external image of the Buddha with the yellow robes and the bump on the top of his head, but more to the realisation of our own true nature.

So that's going for refuge to Buddha, Dharma, and Sangha. Now let's discuss it together a little bit. Do you have any questions?

Discussion

Questioner: You talked about the Buddha and Dharma in terms of inner and outer refuges. Please could you say more about the Sangha in terms of inner refuge?

Rinpoche: When you say Buddha in terms of inner refuge, I think maybe you mean the Buddha within, or the awakening of the Buddha within; while by outer Buddha maybe you mean the historical Buddha, the external

Buddha. When we talk about the Dharma, I don't know whether we can really say inner and outer; it's more like the teaching Dharma and the experience Dharma. Then when we talk about the Sangha, it includes the ultimate or Arya Sangha, meaning those who have the actual experience or realisation, which would include even the Buddha, and then the outer Sangha, which would be the monks and nuns. There's a saying that where there are four monks or nuns there is a Sangha; although that's not really called the outer Sangha, but more the representation of the Sangha. It's not necessarily really the Sangha; the real Sangha consists of the beings who have the experience, the Arya Sangha.

Q: Could you talk about what is meant by going for refuge to the Lama?

R: Yes; we find this in Vajrayana Buddhism. First you go for refuge to the Lama, then Buddha, Dharma, and Sangha. Also in the Vajrayana we find the Lama, Yidam, and Khandro as objects of refuge, but I don't want to make it more complicated by going into that as well! In Vajrayana practice, the Lama becomes very important. But not just any lama! You have to find a good lama, a real lama. But if you find a real lama and then you go for refuge, then the three refuges of Buddha, Dharma, and Sangha are kind of combined in the Lama as an object of refuge. You can say that the Lama's mind is the Buddha, speech is the Dharma, and body is the Sangha. If the Lama has an actual experience of realisation then the mind is like the Buddha; the speech or teaching is the Dharma; and then as the Lama represents the Sangha so the body is the Sangha.

Sometimes it's said that the lama is more important than the buddhas of the three times. That isn't because our lama is more qualified than the Buddha. Our lama isn't really a buddha like Buddha Shakyamuni, but our lama is so important to us because we gain whatever experience we may have through his teaching.

I think this is important to mention. When we say, 'I go for refuge to the Lama,' and we think of our root lama as being so very important to us and so very kind to us, we should understand that how we feel about our lama depends on how much we've been able to benefit from his teaching. Because, as I said before, the Buddha is the teacher, the one who gives the Dharma; so if we have received teaching from the lama, and through that teaching we have really benefited, really gained some experience and understanding and transformation, then naturally we'll have more gratitude and devotion to the lama because we have changed due to his teaching. It's not that we're somehow obliged to see the lama as a buddha; it's just that devotion naturally grows due to the benefit we feel we've received.

It's sometimes said in Vajrayana that your progress in the Dharma shows in how much devotion you have for your guru: the more you have progressed in your Dharma practice the more devotion you will naturally have for your guru, because as your experience deepens so your confidence in your guru becomes stronger. There's a story about the great Tibetan yogi, Milarepa, and his student Gampopa. When Gampopa had finished his studies and was going away, Milarepa said to him: 'Now you must go away and practise meditation. There will come a time when you will see me, your old father Milarepa, as a real buddha. Then you can start teaching, because that will be the sign that you have actually experienced the result of the practice.' So when you start seeing your own teacher as somebody really like a buddha, that means that you yourself have gained some experience of the Dharma. That's what it means in the Vajrayana when we talk about going for refuge to the Lama. But it doesn't apply to every lama who's wearing robes!

Q: Please would you say something about the benefits of taking refuge?

R: I always say that when you have taken the decision to go to a lama to take refuge in a refuge ceremony, actually you have already taken refuge. Unless you are just doing it because others are doing it! But if you feel that you'd like to work on this path and you have some confidence that there is the possibility of development, that's actually the refuge, right there. Then when you go and take refuge in a ceremony it's like finalising your decision, putting the stamp on it. Taking refuge is like finding a direction, a way to go that's good for you and good for others; that's the main understanding. So when you go to a lama to take refuge formally then you're confirming that.

It's also a kind of reminder. As I mentioned earlier, we human beings are not very stable: today we're thinking clearly and we say to ourselves, 'This is the direction I want to take; this is good for me and good for others and I want to do this,' but then tomorrow we forget about it, and within a few days we're doing all sorts of things which we know we shouldn't be doing! So this act of taking refuge is like a reminder. Traditionally we recite the refuge prayer every day, and before doing any Buddhist practice or positive action, and that's a practice in itself; so as we find ourselves forgetting our resolve and becoming caught up in our usual habitual tendencies, we can remind ourselves that we have a direction, a purpose, and a path; we're not just killing time.

So I think the most important benefit of taking refuge is this: it serves as a point of remembrance, so we can remind ourselves that, 'I took refuge from that lama in that place on that day. I decided then that this is the direction I want to take and this is what I want to do.' And that's what practice is, isn't it? It's reminding us of a certain understanding again and again, so that it becomes our habit. And according to the Buddhist understanding our karma – our positive and negative actions – is nothing but habit. So I think the most important benefit of taking refuge is to remind us of our direction. We recite the refuge prayer each day and at the beginning of any practice, and it reaffirms our inspiration.

Q: Could you say something about Mahayana refuge, specifically?

R: I don't think there's too much difference in terms of Mahayana refuge, except this: you're saying, 'I want to become enlightened for the benefit of myself and all sentient beings.' The intention or aspiration in the

Mahayana is to benefit all beings. It's much more strongly inspired by compassion.

Q: It's moving into bodhichitta?

R: Yes. And actually bodhichitta and refuge at the Mahayana level are more or less the same.

Q: If someone is keen to take refuge and wants to finalise it by actually taking refuge with a teacher, and if the person has developed some of the bodhichitta aspiration already and is taking refuge in a Mahayana way, is it good to take the bodhisattva vows at the same time or very soon afterwards, with not much of a gap? Would that be encouraged?

R: Usually when you take refuge, you take refuge only; but when you are a Mahayana practitioner you try to take the refuge with the aspiration, as much as possible, of a bodhisattva, so you try to have the aspiration to work for all sentient beings. It isn't exactly the same as taking the bodhisattva vows because bodhisattva vows are quite specific. Whether or not you've taken the bodhisattva vows, you're taking refuge in the Buddha, Dharma, and Sangha for the benefit of all beings, so in a way you're always expressing the refuge commitment and bodhisattva aspiration together. But when it comes to actually formally taking refuge and bodhisattva vows, usually you take refuge first, and then after some time, if you want to, you take bodhisattva vows. Bodhisattva vows are specific precepts, while refuge is more general.

Q: Often when people take refuge with a teacher they are given a refuge name. Do you consider that as another reminder? What about when people have taken refuge and then they couldn't read their name, maybe because it was written in Tibetan, or they couldn't hear it properly, or they lost it or forgot it, and then they're upset because they feel they've lost something important with it? Please say something about the significance of the refuge name.

R: It can differ according to the different traditions, but in the Tibetan Buddhist way when you take refuge you usually receive a name. It represents that you have started a new way of life; it's kind of a beginning; and therefore it can become like a reminder: 'This is my refuge name.' Also the lama cuts a little bit of your hair and that too is significant: it's said that hair is growing on the highest point of your body, so to make an offering of it represents your highest respect. I don't really know how important the name is. Of course names are important for everybody, because we identify with our names, don't we?

I am what my name is, in a way, aren't I? I am known as Ringu Tulku, so if you say, 'You're not Ringu Tulku,' I say, 'Yes I am; I'm Ringu Tulku.' It's not really me, it's just my name; but names are associated with identification, which is very important for us. I think that's why a new name is given. How important it is to an individual depends on how that person takes it. I think it's OK if you're given a name and you don't remember it! You can get another name. There's no need to be too upset because you didn't hear your name well or you received a name that's very difficult to pronounce – then you can change it! Some Tibetan names are very difficult to pronounce for anybody except Tibetans!

Q: If you have already taken refuge once, is it good to take it again, maybe with a different teacher? Are there any benefits to taking refuge many times? And when you take refuge with a teacher, does that mean you have any particular commitment to that teacher?

R: As I said earlier, taking refuge is really about finding a direction in your life. I don't think it has too much to do with the particular teacher. The ceremony of taking refuge differs a little among the different Buddhist traditions, but basically it's the same: you repeat the refuge prayer three times, saying, 'I go for refuge to the Buddha, I go for refuge to the Dharma, I go for refuge to the Sangha,' and that's it. Usually you do this in front of a person who has already taken refuge, but on certain occasions, for example if you can't find such a person, then you can do it in front of an image, or by visualising the Buddha, Dharma, and Sangha in front of you.

There's not very much to it in terms of commitments. Too many do's and don'ts aren't very helpful. We have to follow the path gradually, and we can't expect to do everything we should, right from the beginning. Usually we say that when we have taken refuge in the Buddha, we don't take refuge in worldly deities and worldly objects. To take refuge in something means to take that object as your ultimate goal, and since your goal is to become enlightened it isn't appropriate to take refuge in anything that isn't compatible with that aim.

For example, if we take refuge in wealth, we think money is everything and we believe it can solve all our problems completely. But, although money is very useful, it can't solve all our problems; therefore we can't take refuge in money in the sense of making possessing material wealth our ultimate goal. But that isn't to say we shouldn't have any money!

The main commitment concerning the Dharma refuge is to try to help others as much as we can, and if we can't help them then at least we try not to harm them. That's the essence of the Dharma, to try to help others.

And the main commitment regarding taking refuge in the Sangha is to try to encourage not only ourselves but also others to go in a positive direction, to bring ourselves and others under a positive influence; and even if we can't do that then we try to avoid being influenced in a harmful way. The point with this last one is not that we don't talk to people who have bad habits, but that we try not to adopt their bad habits ourselves!

Usually in the Tibetan tradition we take refuge from a lama just once in a ceremony as I described, including hair cutting and name giving. Then we repeat the refuge verse again and again, every day throughout our lives, at the beginning of every practice we do, but we don't take refuge again in another formal ceremony.

Thank you all very much.

Dedication

All my chatter in the name of the Dharma
has been set down faithfully
by my dear students of pure vision.

I pray that at least a fraction of the wisdom
of those enlightened teachers who tirelessly trained me
may shine through the mass of my incoherence.

May this help to dispel the darkness of unknowing
in the minds of all beings
and lead them to complete realisation, free from all fear.

Ringu Tulku Rinpoche

Ringu Tulku was born in 1952. He was recognised at an early age as the reincarnation of the abbot of Rigul Monastery in Kham, Eastern Tibet, but has lived since childhood in Sikkim.

Rinpoche has received an extensive traditional training, studying with lamas of all four Tibetan orders. His root lamas were the 16th Gyalwa Karmapa and Dilgo Khyentse Rinpoche. He has also pursued an academic career, receiving the Acarya degree from the Central Institute of Tibetan Higher Studies at Varanasi and being awarded the title of Lopon Chenpo (equivalent to a PhD) by the International Nyingma Society for his research work on Jamgon Kongtrul the Great and the Rimay movement. He was Professor of Tibetology at the University in Gangtok, Sikkim, for 17 years. Among his published books are The Rimay Philosophy of Kongtrul and a series of books for children, written in Tibetan; and, in English, an illustrated book for children: The Boy who had a Dream, and the two booklets which precede this one in the **Lazy Lama** series: Buddhist Meditation, and The

Four Noble Truths. There is also a collection of Tibetan folktales retold by Rinpoche and translated into German under the title Das Juwel des Drachen: Maerchen aus Tibet.

Fluent in English and with a friendly, accessible teaching style, Rinpoche is now in great demand to teach at Western Dharma centres of all the Tibetan traditions.

Bodhicharya

A Non-profit Educational and Cultural Association

"Awaken the Heart by Opening the Mind"

The **Lazy Lama** booklets are published under the auspices of Bodhicharya, a non-profit association registered in Belgium. Founded in 1997 under the direction of Ringu Tulku with the aim of providing a forum for dialogue and learning, Bodhicharya facilitates contact and co-ordination between Rinpoche's friends and students in different countries. Current Bodhicharya activities include collecting, transcribing, translating, and publishing Buddhist teachings and educational materials, and supporting educational and healthcare projects in Tibet.

If you would like to receive further information, please contact:

The Secretary
Bodhicharya
Rue d'Edimbourg 23
1050 Brussels
Belgium

Tel/Fax: +32 2 514 1449
E-mail: co-ordination-office@bodhicharya.org
Website: http://www.bodhicharya.org